I HEART

HEAVEN

I HEART HEAVEN

A PSYCHOTHERAPIST'S
BIBLICAL VALIDATION FOR
NEAR-DEATH EXPERIENCES

TRACY H. GOZA, PH.D.

credo
house publishers

Published in the United States by Credo House Publishers,
a division of Credo Communications, LLC, Grand Rapids, Michigan.
www.credohousepublishers.com

Unless otherwise indicated, all Scripture quotations are from
The Holy Bible, New International Version® NIV® Copyright
© 1973, 1978, 1984, 2011 by Biblica, Inc.™ Used by permission.
All rights reserved worldwide.

ISBN: 978-1-62586-299-0

Cover design by Frank Gutbrod
Interior design by Frank Gutbrod
Editing by Donna Huisjen

The people featured in this book were interviewed voluntarily about their
near death experiences and signed releases of information; they were not
in counseling with the author. The names have been changed to protect
their identities.

Printed in the United States of America
Second edition

CONTENTS

CHAPTER ONE

FOREVER CHANGED

What is a near-death experience (NDE)?

Why should we take them seriously?

How does the Bible relate to NDEs?

The questions begin . . .

n 1985 Carol was a vibrant, 27-year-old trauma nurse who was studying to become a nurse anesthetist. One day she was rushed into urgent surgery for a ruptured ovarian cyst, at the very hospital in which she was a student in training. The surgery began with an initial, light dose of anesthesia, administered by someone Carol had worked with and studied under. The anesthesia dose proved to be too light for Carol, and the pain was excruciating—so terrible she felt compelled to leave her body.

And so began her near-death experience (NDE).

Once out of her body and at that point unaware of the pain, Carol left the operating table and hovered over her body, watching the surgery from a vantage point above her left foot. For a short time she was able to hear the surgeon's comments and music selection. Then, suddenly, she was propelled upward headfirst at a breathtaking speed, into a tunnel in an upper corner of the room.

As Carol rushed up the tunnel, her life came back to her in an all-inclusive review. In mere seconds she re-experienced all aspects of her life, including everything negative she had ever done to anyone firsthand, as though these things had instead happened to her. She recognized the harm she had caused others, feeling in herself the physical and emotional pain she had inflicted on them.

The life review ended and the tunnel widened, at what she understood to be the boundary of heaven. Outside the tunnel other beings were present to greet her. Carol found herself basking in a bright, loving light and heard someone announce, "She's early!" The beings, whom she knew to be God's all-knowledgeable representatives, told her there was more life available for her to live on Earth. They radiated and revealed to her much love, truth, and compassion, as well as what was ahead for her, should she choose to return. Knowledge was given to her—insights she would find herself remembering in bits and pieces later on in life as they unfolded before her, happening in real time. At that point Carol was able to gaze into heaven while assimilating great knowledge, including the majesty of the universe, and unrepeatable insight into the workings of God.

After a time she slowly, but obediently, turned headfirst, back down the tunnel. On the return trip her speed slowed considerably, and Carol could see other tunnels or catacombs flashing by, passageways that branched off from the middle one she was in. She stopped and became aware of shadowy, lifeless beings exuding deceit and ill-will, milling about, watching her, illuminated only by the distant light from heaven.

One of them communicated without speaking, "You can stay here with us."

No, she thought. *I can't stay here with these people; they're dead, I have to keep going.* So she told them, "You're dead—you're not even breathing."

One of them commented, "Neither are you."

Terrified, Carol knew they were right. Back in the operating room the nurse anesthetist had disconnected the endotracheal tube from the respirator, the air had rushed out, and she hadn't taken her first breath on her own yet. Terrified and still partially paralyzed from the anesthesia, and with none of her own breath, she could feel them tapping her sternum to stimulate breathing. Fighting with all her might, she tried to move and breathe to show the operating room personnel that she was in fact alive. Confused by what she had just experienced, and knowing this was unusual based on her years of being an operating room nurse, Carol thought she had been on a ventilator in a coma for ten years and that they were "pulling the plug and letting her go," adding to her terror. Her brain was fully aware, but her muscles were still paralyzed.

Shamed into Silence

I met Carol at a book club meeting over the discussion of a popular book on near-death experiences. In the meeting she revealed having had an NDE, and she and I decided to meet outside the group setting to talk about it. A week later, sitting comfortably in her home with coffee and pastries, she admitted that her

NDE had been stored away in her soul for thirty years and rarely shared, with the exception of her husband, then her fiancé, and a few close friends, none of whom, she admitted, wanted to hear her story. All of them had shut her down, and she feared appearing to be crazy, or, worse, religiously self-promoting. Her pastor at the time had told her that she would be if she ever shared her recollection of the experience. She had internalized it all this time because "no one wanted to listen or hear or ask"—until now.

Like many other people who have had NDEs, Carol had been shamed into silence, left to struggle on her own with one of the most personal and profound psychological events anyone can experience. Carol's whole life had changed after the event. Needing more time to physically recover and to psychologically and emotionally process what had happened, she asked the department head for a personal leave from the anesthetist program; her request was denied. Greatly depressed and traumatized, Carol saw no choice but to withdraw from the program. She continued in nursing but ultimately got married, had children, and ended up staying at home with them.

Now a chaplain at a hospital, Carol describes her NDE and the life changes resulting from it in a positive manner. She is adamant that her life would not have been as meaningful had her career path not changed, and that many wonderful things she has experienced, such as starting a Bible ministry and facilitating a Christian bull-riding school, would not have come to pass had God not spoken to her through her NDE.

As a nurse, Carol desires for others to know that in general anesthetics are safe and that her situation was physically unusual. She believes that God allowed her NDE to draw her closer to himself, and she is trying to stay faithful in her choices to serve God.

Why Study NDEs?

I developed an interest in near-death experiences when, in the master's program and later on in the doctoral program for counseling at the University of North Texas, I met and chose to study under Dr. Janice Miner Holden, department chair, professor in counseling and higher education, and a leading researcher in the field of NDEs. In my studies I have researched and published on NDEs, specifically combat-related, read hundreds of NDE accounts, and personally heard more than I can count through friends and NDErs at conferences on NDEs.

You may wonder why a psychotherapist would study NDEs at all. People come to counseling trying to make sense of their lives, spiritually as well as emotionally. As I discovered by listening to their stories, NDEs have a profound impact on people who experience them. Although none of the NDErs in this book were in counseling with me, it was my privilege to help them articulate how their views have shifted since their NDEs and try to help them integrate what has happened to them. Some people change completely as a result of experiencing an NDE, leaving family, friends, and sometimes even themselves at a loss. What once was comfortable and known sometimes becomes uncomfortable and unknown.

As a therapist, I believe that our daily drives and struggles actually stem from existential questions like Why am I here? Is there an overall purpose in my life for the world or for others? Do I have a unique reason to be here? Is there a God? What happens when we die? NDEs address these questions in many ways. NDErs come back changed, really pursuing answers or believing they have found out some of the answers to these big questions. Seeing and hearing about these people's personal and spiritual changes began to affect me personally—and spiritually as well. I wondered what was happening to them and how my spiritual process and religious upbringing might or might not fit with what I was seeing and hearing.

Growing in Faith

Many Christians have deemed NDEs "mystical," "new-age," or "not biblical." The more I studied and grew spiritually, however, the more I became convinced that my faith and beliefs did not seem to conflict with this subject. The more I read the Bible and heard firsthand from NDErs, the more solidified my faith and beliefs became, although rigidity surrounding certain doctrines changed as my eyes and ears were opened to new biblical perspectives. I began to question the practices of my Baptist denomination, as well as some other denominations. Exploring the chasm between what is man-made about religion and what God actually calls us to do through the Bible in worship and faith has been my exciting new journey. There is less religious "black and white" for me, and more comfort in the gray.

The most exciting thing I've gleaned from exploring what the Bible says and what NDErs have seen is the opportunity and promise of an afterlife. Apparently that life can be either wonderful or horrible, and in a large sense we get to choose which of the two we will have. Near-death experiences also often point to a powerful, compassionate God of All, who is *very* intimately concerned about the personal well-being of his children. How God can be both big-picture and personal to me is mind-blowing and terribly exciting. How I used to view God and heaven has changed completely, and I'd like to share how.

How Do NDEs Fit with the Bible?

My purposes in writing this book are many.

Much of it is devoted to exploring the features of NDEs, such as out-of-body experiences (OBEs), tunnels, "The Light," seeing deceased loved ones, meeting a loving and all-powerful religious figure, life reviews, angels, celestial or atmospheric realms, and even hellish places or experiences. I will also discuss the strange or debatable concepts NDEs present to the Christian faith. Although I do not pretend to be a theologian, I demonstrate how even a layperson like me can find fresh insights from Scripture that will help them handle NDEs in a compassionate and careful manner.

Some questions and topics I will discuss include: Are all NDEs biblical and from God? Are all angels, messengers, or visions from God? What is The Light in the NDE? If the NDEr didn't see Jesus, was Jesus there? How can the NDE be "from God" if the person didn't see God or Jesus? If the NDEr went to heaven, will this happen again for them at their final, physical death, especially if the person wasn't a Christian? I've heard of someone having had both pleasant and distressing NDEs, possibly representing both heaven and hell. Which one is waiting for this person at final, physical death? By daring to ask and attempting to answer these questions, I don't declare myself to be the final authority. Instead, I hope to open a frank and valuable—not to mention fascinating!—conversation about what NDEs are and what we may learn from them. You may disagree or take issue with my conclusions. But I invite you into the dialogue, hoping we can learn from each other in a spirit of building one another up in love (1 Thessalonians 5:11).

Where Does the Church Fit In?

Another reason I'm writing this book is to share with churchgoers how NDErs report feeling about trying a new church in their area, and what might be done to rectify the negative aspects of this situation. NDErs have told me they've felt strange, unwelcome, or not religious enough and that they haven't been taken seriously or have been ostracized and confused when they've opened up about their experience at church or tried to find a church home after their experience. This leads many NDErs to spiritual frustration, isolation, and confusion. I believe that churches can change their approach to NDErs through knowledge of and familiarity with the subject, as well as through developing an attitude of compassion rather than of judgment.

Why is it important for NDErs to find a church home? NDErs often report heaven as a place that is "more real" than their previously known reality, with colors and scents beyond what we are aware of in our limited earthly bodies. Their glimpse of heaven gives them a spiritual hunger. They want to learn about this place they saw, so they are open to reading about it in the Bible and often turn to the church as a place where they can find out more. But if their NDE is disregarded, they are likely to turn away from the church in discouragement instead of being nurtured into a biblical faith. My hope in writing about NDEs is that all Christians will welcome into their congregations NDErs and others who have had "nontraditional" spiritual experiences, so that everyone may have a place to grow and learn about God in community.

Finally, how should a Christian church member treat an NDEr or someone else who claims to have had "different," "nontraditional," "nonbiblical," unusual spiritual, or mystical experiences? Many NDErs report feeling isolated by not having a physical church home or place of worship because they have become less religious and more spiritual from their NDEs. Others have been shamed, shunned, or silenced by religious or trusted church members or clergy, or they have not been invited in to share their unique stories and gifts with the community. I'm hoping that, based on this book, this situation will at least begin to change. I will address what someone might do or say to encourage or welcome an NDEr (or someone else sharing mystical or seemingly nonbiblical experiences) into your church, small group, or Sunday school.

Using the Bible as Authority and Filter

This book differs from others on NDEs in that I am filtering my understanding and view of NDEs through the Bible, and not the other way around. I'm doing my best to allow Scriptures and themes of the Bible to maintain their credibility and authority, while still affirming NDEs, despite the fact that other books in the recent past have discounted key Christian principles in order to affirm NDEs. Although concepts in this book regarding Scripture may seem radical or unbiblical, I believe that the concepts I share, based on biblical research, will maintain their biblical accuracy, while allowing space for NDEs. In other words, I do not believe I'm advocating new concepts about the Bible that have never been studied or discussed before. What I am doing is simply sharing my insights about NDEs in light of what I've learned, granting that these ideas may seem new or even strange or unbelievable.

In reality the topic of this book is heaven and hell. There are many theories and feelings about these places. Our God is a big God, and as I grow and learn I am extremely excited about what I present in this book; the information I offer, as well as my carefully researched and thought-out suggestions, leave far more scope in our finite minds for God to be who he is: majestic, loving, just, and sovereign, "outside the box." I'm in awe. My eyes are wide open. As I observe the pieces of this puzzle seemingly fitting together, I get so excited I feel compelled to share.

We can call this book what it is: one researcher's thoughts on NDEs and how they might relate to God, Jesus, heaven, and hell throughout the Bible. Granted, this is just one book in a sea of books on NDEs. But the concepts have changed my life by teaching me more about God's character traits, including his passionate love; limitless creativity; unending wisdom; supremacy; . . . and, yes, even humor! I have been strengthened to trust God and follow Jesus even though I don't understand everything about the heavenly home God has prepared. As I reflect on his promises laid out in the Bible in light of NDEs, my eyes and heart are being increasingly opened to living daily in the heavenly realms. I have been forever changed. I heart heaven.

CHAPTER TWO

NEAR-DEATH EXPERIENCES

WHAT ARE THEY, AND WHERE DO THEY COME FROM?

Current debates over NDEs

Common characteristics of an NDE

Are NDEs from God?

n 1975 a medical student, Raymond Moody, wrote a book titled *Life After Life*, in which he explored the phenomena of what he called near-death experiences. Moody coined the phrase, as well as the acronym NDE. He explained that the recounting of NDEs can be found in ancient writings across cultures. However, for mainstream Americans, many of whom were learning about this phenomenon for the first time, a spiritual, not to mention scientific, can of worms was being opened. Some were fascinated and believed in NDEs; others tossed the fantastical stories aside like junk news. Either way, a legitimate medical opinion had been shared, conversations begun, and scientific studies undertaken. Since then many books have been published on NDEs, and researchers spanning numerous fields have created and published elaborate research projects, either validating or discounting NDEs based on their findings.

Current scientific studies are still locked in debate, with some research suggesting that NDEs are the product of a dying brain and others arguing that the soul (or consciousness) and the brain are different entities, with the brain being able to "die" while the soul lives on.

What Is an NDE?

According to researcher Bruce Greyson, NDEs are "profound psychological events with transcendental and mystical elements, typically occurring to individuals close to death or in situations of intense physical or emotional danger."[1] Technically, if the person was not in any way near death and had their experience while sleeping or praying, the terms "near-death-like experience" or "NDLE" may be used, though for the most part people call them all NDEs.

NDEs can be pleasant or distressing, heavenly and wonderful or hellish and horrible. Some can even be a mix.

During an NDE, people may experience any of the following:

---

1 Etzel Cardena, Steven Jay Lynn, and Stanley Krippner, eds., *Varieties of Anomalous Experience: Examining the Scientific Evidence* (Washington, D.C.: American Psychological Association, 2000), 315-16.

- being out of body
- floating above themselves and observing their body
- feeling carefree or at peace
- entering and/or going through a tunnel
- seeing a bright light at the end
- feeling all-encompassing love in the presence of a bright light
- seeing deceased loved ones
- seeing or communicating with religious figures
- experiencing a life review
- having access to amazing amounts of knowledge about the universe or the future
- experiencing heightened senses and a wider range of colors than perceivable on Earth
- arriving at a border or point of no return
- choosing whether or not to return or being directed to return
- Returning instantaneously back into their bodies or making a return journey

The more of the aspects listed above the person experienced, the "deeper" the NDE is said to have been. However, in my opinion All NDEs are completely significant and life-changing, regardless of their "depth."

NDErs have experienced being in exceptionally beautiful and peaceful pastoral scenes, or standing at gates, with some specifically knowing they were at the "gates of heaven" or "in heaven." Some NDErs find themselves in celestial places in the realm of the moon and stars, in distant galaxies, in voids of space and time, in black holes, in dark recesses of the earth, or in pits, some of which they've specifically described as "hellish places."

Some NDErs have reunited with long-lost pets or experienced an awareness of the presence of former pets. Others have found themselves among crowds of people awaiting their arrival, with some describing crowds of either angels or demons. Some have felt free, while others experienced feeling chained or restricted.

Some NDErs return to their bodies aware of gifts they had not known before, including an ability to contact spirits, read others' minds, or speak to others telepathically. Some report physiological changes, such as not being able to use a watch or maintain a working computer because the electronic devices keep stopping or freezing up.

An NDE is like a snowflake; no two are alike, although many share similarities. Even more interesting to me is that some NDErs who have strange or scary-sounding experiences still describe them in somewhat positive terms. Each NDE is unique in the eye of the beholder, meaning that this individual is the one to process and define it.

Are NDEs from God?

With all of these experiences we must ask ourselves, What is going on? Christians specifically may want to know, Are all these NDEs from God? I see it as critical to address this before moving on. I can hear what you're thinking: Does Tracy really think these experiences are spiritual and not just part of the brain shutting down? People are given lots of medications; couldn't this be some sort of high?

First of all, I do believe that many of these experiences may be "from" God. After many years of studying, praying, researching, and listening to accounts of people's NDEs, I believe that God might be trying to get people's attention through NDEs *in light of how specifically meaningful and uniquely fitting they are to the circumstances of each person*. What the individual does with what they see or hear is up to them (all of us have free will and the ability to make choices), but after hearing how time and again the NDEr saw or felt or heard something that only he or she would recognize or be significantly touched by, I believe that God could be at work in this direct manner. And let me be even clearer by stating what some may take as a given: I believe this to be the God of the Bible.

So what about non-Christians? I believe that God reaches out to millions every day in order that they might come to know and love him. And I believe that many NDEs are "from" God in the sense that he at least allows them to happen and can use them for his purposes. This includes happy as well as horrible NDEs.

I am convinced, however, that some NDEs are *not* "from" God in the sense of having been designed or sent by God, although, as I have just stated, God can and does still use them. Second Corinthians 11:14 speaks about Satan masquerading as a "being of light." We are talking about an exceptionally cunning creature who knows how to dazzle, impress, and impersonate. He knows how to create the façade of life out of death and truth from a complete lie. Some of the NDEs I read about or hear reported seem to fit into this later category—in such cases I would argue that what people are experiencing isn't the peaceful, well-meaning, or heavenly realm they think they're observing but a lie, a façade.

I believe that it's up to the individual NDEr to decide what they believe on a spiritual level was happening to them during the NDE and to seek

out what the Bible has to say to them about it. It is
most definitely not up to me to judge or attempt
to interpret the kind of NDE the person has had.
This is his or her own journey. There is no way I
can know in an individual instance whether the
NDE was "from" God or crafted by Satan, but I do
believe that all NDEs happen for a reason—for a
very specific reason, even—to the precise people
who experience them. In my opinion all NDEs,
whether pleasurable or distressing, offer material
for learning, and their lessons can be applied
directly to life here on Earth.

CHAPTER THREE

ENCOUNTERS WITH THE DIVINE

Is Jesus present in an NDE?

How and why does God reveal

himself in NDEs?

Biker Dennis Shea is a leather-wearing, sixty-five-year-old personal protection officer. A devoted husband and active Christian for the past forty-five years, he sports a long white ponytail and a goatee. His past includes some rebellious early years; at one point he roomed with a member of the Hells Angels, who, incidentally, was "out in bad standings."

The summer evening of August 19, 2010, was beautiful in Texas, and the then sixty-two-year-old took advantage of it by taking his motorcycle out for a ride. A seasoned biker, Dennis chose a back road to I-20. Easing up onto the eastbound interstate, he noted road construction and the absence of a right shoulder, as it was partitioned off by cones.

At first his ride was unremarkable except for the freedom and joy that riding a motorcycle on a beautiful day can afford. Dennis stayed in the right-hand lane, allowing cars and trucks to pass him on the left. But soon he noted that the asphalt was being redone and that his lane had been scraped down, leaving an uneven surface with its telltale wavy lines. Although not a major nuisance for such a seasoned rider, he decided he might prefer to move left to the inside lane where there was a smooth surface.

Road conditions change fast, as does the flow of traffic, and as Dennis was contemplating changing lanes he became aware of an 18-wheeler approaching on his back left and his own lane closing down into the other. Recent eye surgery had left Dennis with corrected 20/20 vision in his right eye, but an eye patch covered the left, decreasing his clear vision by 50 percent. Remembering this, he decided at the last moment that he couldn't make the lane change quickly enough to avoid cutting off the 18-wheeler and endangering himself. Dennis braced himself to ride out the rough pavement as he passed through the cones into the dangerous construction zone.

Suddenly he faced new pavement in his lane— several inches thick with no graded ramp. With no time or room to react, Dennis took a gamble jumping up onto the pavement—a gamble he lost.

Dennis woke up in the ER. He has no memory of police or an ambulance but recalls being in the hospital and aggressively trying to pull the tube of oxygen out of his throat. He recalls being strapped down and thinks the medical personnel had intentionally induced a coma. He sustained head trauma, multiple broken ribs, a collapsed lung, fluid on the lung, pulmonary embolism or a blood clot in the lung, deep vein thrombosis, contusions, a broken clavicle, a severe body rash, and a bruised heart. When he arrived at the hospital he had no blood pressure and wasn't breathing on his own.

Dennis was in a coma for five days and in the hospital for eight. He was given a tracheotomy, and he needed five or six laser surgeries over the next year and a half to correct the scarring in his throat. The accident and tracheotomy left him physically and vocally weaker. At the same time, the NDE he experienced strengthened him.

Jesus came to Dennis in his coma. They were sitting together in a coffee shop at a small table with two chairs. Jesus was dressed casually in a lightweight, zippered golf jacket, a polo shirt, and khakis; he was so ordinary looking that no one would have pointed him out in a crowd.

Jesus asked Dennis, "So, what do you want to do now?" With a smirk, Dennis asked what his options were. Jesus answered, "Well, you can come with me now or you can come with me later. It's up to you."

Dennis said, "Lord, if it's really all the same to you, I just want to go with you now, but I still have some things to do here, people depending on me."

Jesus agreed, "I still have some things for you to do too." And with that, Jesus stood up and walked out.

It was several months before Dennis told his wife about the NDE, and she wondered aloud when it might have happened during the five days he was in a coma. He told her it was during the second or third night, when the doctors were uncertain whether he was going to live. Hearing his story, his wife became excited and began crying. She told him that she had been praying over him, pleading with God over his life, and that God had replied to her prayer and impressed upon her that it was up to her to decide whether he were to live or die. She was given a decision to make, just as Jesus had given it to Dennis in the NDE. She had fervently prayed, sharing with God humorously, "Lord, you know there were times I wanted to kill him . . ." but that she really wanted him to live.

In that moment Dennis and his wife realized that God had been working both ends of the deal and that the experience on both their parts had been valid. Since his NDE, Dennis has continued ministering through the Circuit Riders Motorcycle Ministry, which puts him in touch with the families of downed bikers. He visits and prays with them. Dennis stated, "I have since been in several of these hospital scenarios, and I can reassure the families: Jesus still does business when people are in a coma."

When asked why he thought Jesus might have presented himself in such a casual way at a coffee shop, Dennis replied, "Because I'm casual! I often wear jeans to church."

Dennis credits the Lord with many positive life changes since his accident and NDE. He states that the trauma of being injured and the stress of paying high medical bills were a small price to pay for the joy he experiences in ministering to others and telling them of his encounter with Jesus while he was in a coma. He is grateful to be for the most part healed and to have a testimony he can share with other bikers.

Encounters with the Divine

Dennis is a Christian who was blessed with an NDE that included an encounter with Jesus. Not everyone who experiences an NDE will have such a personal encounter. However, many recall a bright light or a voice or some other entity they identify as a divine being. Is that light or voice or entity God or Jesus? And if so, why does God reveal himself in this way, especially to nonbelievers?

Let me start by stating the obvious: an NDE is *not* final death and is *not* even necessarily what will happen to the same person at final death. This is important to note because I believe God allows people glimpses of what they need to see or what he wants them to see in their NDE, while there is time left in their lives to impact their character, future earthly life, and afterlife. Sometimes they receive a promise, sometimes a warning. Either way, this encounter with the divine is extremely powerful to the NDEr, a crucial part of their spiritual story. I think it has everything to do with God revealing himself not only to the person but to the present generation.

The Bible states clearly that unbelievers, or people who do not put their faith in Jesus Christ, will not go to heaven. Jesus declared, "I am the way and the truth and the life. No one comes to the Father except through me" (John 14:6). So, people wonder, how can an unbeliever claim they have seen Jesus and heaven (where God dwells) in their NDE? Or how can someone claim they never saw or knew Jesus but did see God?

All throughout the Bible God reveals himself over and over again to people, Christian or not, encouraging them to follow him. I don't see this as disputed, and it isn't a huge leap to imagine that a non-Christian might have an NDE and meet a divine figure and see heaven in a God-given attempt to let the unbeliever experience biblical truth.

Here's how I think this can happen. If Jesus is always the intermediary, the go-between, the missing link that allows a person to experience God—which is clearly shown in the Bible as truth—then why do we assume with regard to these "I saw God or I felt God or I heard God" NDEs that Jesus wasn't also there? What if he was and is? Just because the person didn't see or notice Jesus to recall him doesn't mean that the Son wasn't present. Also, just because Jesus was there in the NDE and didn't look like what everyone thinks he should look like doesn't mean it wasn't Jesus.

Look up in a concordance the instances of the word *light* as used to describe Jesus or God.

The analogy or imagery appears multiple times. Jesus declares himself to be the Light of the world (John 8:6). In 1 Timothy 6:16 God is declared to be immortal and said to live in "inapproachable light." Jesus turns darkness into light in 1 Peter 2:9, and God himself is equated with light in 1 John 1:5.

I believe that unbelievers, those not having had a prior belief in Christ, could have their (not-final-death) NDE and "see" or experience God without having seen Jesus because Jesus may actually have been there as The Light. I have heard and read hundreds of accounts of NDEs. Many of the NDErs describe encountering the most incredibly loving Light that *knew their souls and gave them peace.* A Light with a body or a form without a face. A Light who really knew who they were, every aspect of them and all they had done, . . . and loved them anyway. People felt at home in The Light. They felt embraced by it and never wanted to leave it. People felt loved and judged to be human and still loved some more. People experienced watching their life's review with The Light and were encouraged to do better.

People felt the remorse of hurting others, but The Light helped them through the agony and showed them the possibilities of their futures. This Light people are experiencing in their NDEs certainly has the character qualities of Jesus. Of Jesus loving them and knowing them, judging their acts and still redeeming them.

By way of clarification, I'm not saying that The Light *always* is Jesus. I'm just sharing the possibility that an NDEr who does not believe in Jesus could experience the presence of God the Father in their NDE because The Light—being Jesus—ushered them there. If Jesus is still the intermediary, the scenario can still be biblical. Who am I to say that The Light in the NDE couldn't be Jesus or that Jesus doesn't reveal himself to people when they came back from their NDEs? Many people have experienced NDEs with events or strange details in them that didn't make sense until they played out later on in real time, leaving them to marvel or seek more information.

Who Did They See?

But why would Jesus or even God in these NDEs not look like themselves or reveal themselves definitively as God? Why wouldn't Jesus make himself known?

Once again, note the many instances in the Bible in which Jesus was not recognized as himself, even to people exceptionally close to him who should have known what he looked and sounded like. Mary Magdalene, after Jesus' death and burial, stood and spoke with him, thinking he was the gardener (John 20:13). Two believers walked with Jesus on the road to Emmaus, "but they were kept from recognizing him" (Luke 24:16). In both cases Jesus was talking with people he knew—in Mary's case intimately—and loved and they didn't recognize him, possibly because they didn't expect to see him (after all, they thought he had died) but also because Jesus prevented them from recognizing him. Jesus did clear up any confusion, and his identity didn't stay hidden from them, but just because he revealed himself fairly quickly doesn't make his presence void if in other instances he opts not to do so within the time frame or manner someone expects.

Some might argue that, if Jesus had been The Light or in some other unrecognizable form in the NDE, he would certainly have cleared up his identity or purposes within the event. However, the Bible shows us that God reveals himself in his own timing. Noah took 100 years to build the ark in a desert where people had seldom seen rain. Moses waited in the desert for forty years for God's answers and promise. Abraham was more than 100 years old when Isaac was born. God may not instantly reveal himself or his plans, but he will not remain hidden. The Bible says that those who seek him will find him (Proverbs 8:17).

Three Wise Chinese Men

I was startled once when an NDEr described his encounter with the divine as being with three Chinese wise men. Nothing in my Southern Baptist upbringing had prepared me for that image of God! However, on further reflection and study of Scripture, I recalled the story of the Lord appearing to Abraham in the form of three men standing near his tent (Genesis 18:1). In the account Abraham greets them graciously and feeds them, and one of them declares that Abraham's wife will have a baby in one more year. After reading this I abandoned all angst at hearing an NDEr describe God as "three wise Chinese men."

I have heard NDErs describe God as a loving voice; as a person known to them that in a given moment was actually Jesus; and even as a nondescript person among many who spoke to them and they somehow *knew* it was actually God. In the Bible God appeared as a burning bush to Moses, a "man" whom Jacob wrestled, and pillars of cloud and fire to the Israelites. Their stories and the stories in Scripture convince me that God can reveal himself in any form he chooses. If someone says they saw God, I believe them. It isn't my call to contest their account or their conclusion. Can't someone "see" God in the form God chooses to share himself and it not be his actual "face," which the Bible clearly states no one can see (John 1:18 and 6:46)? Taking the argument still further, aren't God's references to his face, or hands or eyes or feet merely a convention to meet us at a point of comprehension our limited knowledge can grasp? Can NDErs not receive a feeling, a picture, or an intelligent and soul-searching grasp on who God is through whatever it is they saw depicted as God? I believe they can. At this point, hopefully you too can see how I am convinced that an unbeliever who had experienced a (not final death) NDE without seeing Jesus (possibly depicted as The Light) could still have "seen" or experienced God.

Can I know these things for sure? No. Can I rest assured that the three wise Chinese men were God? No. Can we say that Jesus wasn't there just because the person didn't see or describe him or even know about him? No. Should we trash all NDEs as garbage that Christians should rebuke and steer clear of? Absolutely not! In further chapters I will explain why I believe NDEs have something to teach not only those who experience them but all of us reading and hearing about them in the here and now, on this side of heaven.

CHAPTER FOUR

THE JOYS OF A NEAR-DEATH EXPERIENCE

Characteristics of a happy near-death experience

Why is an NDE often such a positive experience?

Could a positive NDE result in

false confidence or faulty beliefs?

Helen, a retired educator from Texas and a cherished family friend, had an NDE after having major surgery. Scheduled for a spinal fusion in her lower back, she prayed about it and felt ready for the three-hour-long process. Her husband, children, and some extended family members and friends camped out in the waiting room, emotionally supporting and praying for her.

All had gone well, according to the surgeon, but the medical personnel were having difficulty awakening Helen. Instead of her being transferred to a recovery room one to two hours later, the process took four to five hours—but not without something miraculous intervening. While her family waited, anxiously aware of her post-surgical difficulty, Helen lay unaware of their disturbance. Instead she found herself standing in a perfect place, a beautiful, breathtaking meadow with luscious green rolling hills.

"It felt like this was home," she told me. "Immediately I felt like I had gone home. It was perfect! Total safety, peace, and joy." Helen knew that this place was exactly where she had always wanted to be, although she had never been there before. She admired the tiny yellow flowers and robin's-egg blue sky, sensing that it all felt completely and totally familiar. The only word she could come up with to describe the place she saw was "clarity." Total clarity, as though all of it were distinct and perfect, vivid and sharp, with perfected abilities even bestowed upon her senses. With her heightened awareness she could see every individual blade of emerald grass and could feel upon her cheek a breeze so gentle it felt like a caress.

Down a slope below her were perfect trees by a gently flowing river. She marveled that there were no dead leaves on the trees and that the water was crystal clear. "It may have had a hue to it, but it was like looking through a clear marble," she remembered. The smooth water flowed effortlessly, sometimes over rocks, and she found herself thinking, "I'm gonna go over there," intuitively sensing that her "destination" was on the other side of that mesmerizing river.

Along with the sense of the familiar, a soothing sound, like humming, caught her attention. "Either it was the wind or the water, but it wasn't just one tone. It was like a melody. It wasn't distinct, but it felt like soothing music."

Helen laughed and confessed, "This is the silly part. I then looked over to my left and was so excited because I expected to see my childhood dog running to me. I just knew he was coming to greet me." He had been given to her when she was five and died when she was sixteen. She was filled with delight that she would be seeing him again.

Unfortunately, but seemingly in perfect timing, Helen experienced people patting her and then almost slapping her arms and face. She aroused only enough to tell the nurses how beautiful everything was in that moment and that she wanted to go back. They urged her with more patting, telling her that she couldn't go back and asking her to wake up and join them in the room. Once fully awake, Helen kept telling them how beautiful the place had been; she even confided in one nurse that death would be okay because it was so beautiful and peaceful.

Helen still maintains that she has zero concerns about passing out of this world when it's her time to go. "Physical pain isn't fun. I've pretty much been in pain ever since then, but I want to shake people and say, if you're a believer in Christ and he has invited you home, he will take you somewhere far more wonderful."

She shared that she had been deeply disappointed at having to return. "What I saw was more beautiful than any earthly beauty. I still get excited about it. I'm not looking forward to more pain and aging, but I'm really looking forward to the part that comes after. All we have to do is accept Christ's invitation."

Characteristics of a Happy NDE

I don't know how many pleasurable NDEs there are to every distressing one, because distressing or hellish experiences are underreported (the next chapter will report on a few). However, there are many wonderful aspects of pleasurable NDEs. Our society, myself included, can't seem to hear enough of these heavenly pleasures.

The pleasurable aspects of NDEs often (but not always) include:

- Realization of leaving the body and existing beyond it, absence of physical pain, and acceptance of this phenomenon with peace
- Awareness of beautiful new realms, such as heavenly pastoral places; celestial places with planets, stars, or wide open spaces; or cities with people, angels, or other spiritual beings
- Reception by a bright and exceptionally loving light or by spiritual beings
- Reunion with family, friends, or pets
- Undergoing a life review

Awareness that people report in their NDEs includes:

- Feeling intense love, acceptance, peace, a sense of being whole or complete, feeling

new or perfect, feeling at home or feeling one with everything
- The sense of a body made whole and perfect; renewed abilities with the capability of far more than earthly enablement; awareness of free will or choice with regard to certain specified outcomes, past or future events; or a return to the body
- Amazing insight gleaned during the NDE, with partial or full retention of that knowledge and possibly special messages for loved ones
- Acceptance of or affirmation of spirituality, religious faith, beliefs

We will look at these emotional, spiritual, and intellectual responses to NDEs later in the book. But with a list like this, who wouldn't get excited! I sometimes call this response "NDE Envy," wishing for such a wonderful experience with all of its amazing insights—without a tragic, scary, or painful event leading up to it, of course.

For now, let's take a look at some of the positive elements commonly found in NDEs and what makes these unusual experiences so pleasurable—even when to the outside observer they may appear frightening!

Out-of-Body Experience, Absence of Pain, and Feelings of Peace

Most NDEs begin with an out-of-body experience accompanied by an absence of pain. One would think that finding oneself floating outside one's body would induce fear or panic, but for most people the experience is pleasant, peaceful, and even joyful. NDErs often feel immediate peace as they leave behind the struggles of life or death and are able to focus on a new way of being. NDErs enjoy the absence of pain and swiftly accept what is happening to them.

David, a retired middle school geography teacher, had an OBE after collapsing during a Labor Day fundraising race. He "viewed" himself lying in the hospital bed, found himself in the presence of "voices in shimmering white robes," and was filled with such a wonderful sensation of peace that he didn't want to go back to his body. While he was in the presence of the voices, he was informed that this was not his time and that he would have to return. David recalled his almost four-year-old daughter and his infant daughter, both of whom, he knew, needed him. He was almost pushed forcibly back, he recalls, because he didn't want to leave that incredible peace.

Awareness of Beautiful New Realms

NDErs often encounter stunningly beautiful or unique surroundings, and I get chills of excitement listening to their attempts at describing what they saw. Over and over again NDErs strain to explain colors or shapes or places they saw, only to come up short or speechless, held captive by unforgettable images and feelings beyond the scope of the human imagination. People may describe odd events in their NDEs that we might explain as *synesthesia*, a union of the senses. They may view events that trigger flashes of colors or feel smells or see word pictures of thoughts. Graphic and meaningful to the NDEr, these experiences are most alluring, reminding me that the afterlife can be so much more brilliant, creative, and intriguing than my earthly mind can fathom. This is thrilling to me.

Sometimes people find themselves in gorgeous meadows or on rolling hillsides. We might jokingly call these spaces the outskirts of heaven. Other times people find themselves at gates or by walls, sensing themselves to be just outside the entrance to heaven. For some the space is just a heavenly aura consisting of amazing bright hues. For others the scene is more celestial, and they are suspended in a galaxy or amongst thousands of bright stars. While dangling in space might sound scary to the listener, the NDEr can find the experience pleasurable, and even heavenly, especially if they are buoyed by a sensation of feeling loved or have the sense that they are gaining insight. The pleasures of an NDE really depend upon the response of the person having it.

People have seen cities in NDEs as well. While cities are often viewed from afar, one NDEr had a close-up look, as described on the website www.NDERF.com. "Gregory W" shares details of a city within high, solid stone walls that were transparent, much like glass. He shares depictions of gold streets and of twelve different colors he would not have seen on Earth, as he is colorblind. His NDE is fascinating, and not unusual. Cities have been described as translucent, beautiful, having brilliant colors beyond our human color spectrum, and being made up of jewels or light. In addition, some NDErs see or sense people in the city.

The Light, Jesus, or Spiritual Beings

The previous chapter already looked at this aspect of an NDE. Of all the positive attributes of an NDE, The Light is the most fascinating to many who experience it. Described in countless similar ways, most often it is so intense that it would hurt human eyes, though it doesn't affect those of the

NDEr, and often it exudes all-encompassing love to the individual. Many NDErs believe this light to be the Creator of the universe or God.

Jesus's presence, if recognizable either as The Light or apart from it, is also a source of joy. Many NDErs, like Dennis, know who he is without being told and in his presence sense an unworthiness that is not shame-inducing because it is overridden by a worthiness on the basis of the sacrifices Jesus has made for them. This newfound or reclaimed worthiness often leads to confidence, purpose, a more intense love for others, and underlying joy upon their return.

Spiritual beings or angels often accompany NDErs. Both are at times described as being "guides," and many do literally guide the person through the unknown spiritual territory. NDErs often report the guides as angels having wings, but other guides may be seen as people. In some cases the guides turn out to be never-met-before or not-remembered siblings or other relatives, which can bring the NDEr an overwhelming sense of comfort, joy, and peace, especially upon their return and reflection upon the NDE. Sometimes these guides are described as "orbs of light" or just "voices," both of which can still be a source of comfort and joy to the NDEr.

Joyful Reunion with Deceased Loved Ones

One sunny afternoon I went with my family to visit my elderly aunt and several cousins at my aunt's home in the countryside of East Texas. Tiny and frail, but with sparkling eyes, she recounted to us something that had happened to her while undergoing knee surgery months earlier. Coffee pouring stopped, as did all side conversations. We all sat and listened intently.

In her barely audible, wavering voice she began, "All of a sudden, I was at the gates and they wouldn't let me in!" She claimed that she spotted her long-deceased husband of sixty-five years and that "he looked great!" Then she said she had seen my grandmother, who had passed away years earlier, moving toward her with a message for my still-living grandfather. Just before my grandmother could give her the message, my aunt was back in her body.

I sat stunned—thrilled and annoyed all at the same time. Why couldn't my grandmother have shared her message faster! My aunt was clearly serious about what she had experienced, however, and I was elated. To this day I can imagine what NDErs might feel when they get to a heavenly place and reunite with a loved one, or if they are sent a specific message from a heaven-dweller. Excitement and anticipation fill me each time I think of this wonderful story. Since then my elderly aunt has passed away, as has my grandfather, and I can only imagine the reunion they all shared when they finally arrived.

As a therapist I am often privileged to counsel with people as they mourn the loss of loved ones. When I hear the stories of joyful reunions that take place in many NDEs, I'm reminded that the ecstasy of reunion isn't limited to my own personal reuniting with family, friends, or pets but can also include the joy of "witnessing" the reunions of others! Many NDErs describe crowds of people waiting for them, people they didn't know previously as well as loved ones. Nothing brings out my NDE excitement more than anticipating reunifications of all sorts, and the healing that will come with being together again with our loved ones and those others who jubilantly welcome our presence.

The Life Review

One might think a life review would be intimidating or depressing, but for most NDErs it becomes a source of great joy after they get over their initial apprehension. In a life review an NDEr views the events of their life almost as in movie form. Some people stand with The Light or with a spiritual guide beside them as they review their life and the emotions it evokes—all of its contentment and anger, joys and sorrows. The NDEr often senses the impact of their actions upon others and empathizes with others' resulting emotions of hurt or anger. NDErs will observe and accept those areas in which they should have acted differently or ways in which their actions have caused a ripple effect, either positive or negative. The life review is incredibly profound to the NDEr.

Indeed, the life review aspect of the NDE is amazing to me every time I hear accounts of it. I deem myself to be in an incredibly privileged position each time I'm invited to witness the astounding impact of a life review on the NDEr. The life review—even with the negatives that are brought to light—is such a positive experience, I believe, because it helps NDErs feel "known" and "tracked" by God. Often The Light talks them through the review and reveals insight about change or grace, allowing them to come out of the review feeling loved, acknowledged, and free to keep on living. In addition, the review often jump-starts renewal or rebirth in an NDEr's life.

Interestingly, I have never read or heard a life review in which the person described a wonderful sequence of events with no need to change any aspects of their encounters with others and with

no feelings of regret—in other words, a review in
which The Light says only "Great job."

However, I have observed many accounts in
which, after the person's life review, (complete
with life lessons to be learned or regrets) the
NDEr reports not feeling admonished or pushed
by The Light to do better, but rather energized
and free from guilt, regret, or remorse. This
freedom can be a source of happiness for the
NDEr, motivating them to make changes for the
better in their lives. Sadly, however, it may also
help them rationalize or justify continuing to live
however they wish.

A life review in an NDE could be interpreted
by a Christian as a personal judgment. While
not being the final death experience, the NDE
might still be a foreshadowing of personal,
biblical judgment for the specific NDErs who
have experienced it. The Bible states clearly that
all people will be held accountable to God for
their actions (see 1 Peter 4:5). Positive actions are
evidence of a faith in God but do not in and of
themselves constitute faith in God, nor will good

actions save the individual. Only Christ himself can save (Romans 3:22–24). While an NDEr's life review may occur in the context of love and compassion, as they often do, it is not, according to the Bible, confirmation of God's final decision for where they will go after death (see Revelation 20:11–15).

False Confidence in a Heavenly Afterlife

Can a pleasurable NDE result in false confidence in a heavenly afterlife? In other words, does experiencing or even hearing about the joys of near-death experiences make us tend to believe that almost everyone is going to heaven, even if that might not be true? If this question seems unsettling to you, you aren't alone. I've wrestled and wrestled with it. Unfortunately, I believe the answer is yes. I'm proposing three possible ways in which a person could experience and respond to a joyful NDE, two of which could lead to faulty confidence in a heavenly afterlife. Recall that I am filtering these beliefs through what I believe the

Bible says about heaven and hell. Before you bail out, however, also know that I do believe there is a large gray area here, with far less black and white than we recognize surrounding what we think we know about salvation and the afterlife; I'll explain later in the book.

I firmly believe that there is ample evidence of life after death, both on the basis of the biblical teachings that tell us about it and people's personal accounts. I am not concerned that NDErs and others will be misled into thinking there is some sort of afterlife when there actually isn't. The question for the individual is, rather, whether the afterlife for them will be pleasant or distressing. Heavenly or hellish.

A Taste of the Afterlife that Falls Short

The first possibility is that God allows NDEs to give people a taste of an afterlife that will be filled with indescribable wonders. This seems to be what a lot of people do experience. The sad possibility is that the NDEr may come back thinking all is well, that they can proceed to heaven when the time is right without changing their beliefs, their lifestyles, or their character. Or, like many NDErs, they may come back remarkably changed (as most are) and live out their remaining time with new purpose and conviction (as most feel compelled to do), *without also taking* the crucial step of inviting Jesus into their lives. At final death they may very well realize that a relationship with Jesus is missing and that they will not in fact be destined for heaven. What a tragedy! I don't want this to happen to anyone. In fact, one of the major reasons I am writing this book is to invite NDErs to take that vital step of seeking out a relationship with Jesus.

Most people want to believe that everyone is going to heaven when they die, except for maybe Hitler and some other notoriously evil people. I believe, with them, that God truly *wants* to save all humankind (John 3:17). But I do not believe this will actually happen, because many people will and do choose to reject his Son, Jesus.

The Bible says that living eternally in heaven, where God dwells, is *only* done through one understanding and accepting the free gift of grace from a perfect God to imperfect humans through his son, Jesus (John 3:16-21).

A Deception from Satan

A second possible way in which I envision someone having a pleasurable NDE and coming away deceived is arguably even more unsettling. Some NDErs may view a heavenly place that is a fraud and a sham, a spectacular deception perpetrated by Satan. Yes, I'm proposing that Satan could craft a pleasurable NDE, full of light, love, all-powerful spiritual beings, and beautiful voices sharing wisdom. No one wants to believe that such a beautiful experience, one in which the person might even be "certain" they have spoken with God, might be a complete deception. How could Satan do this and why? It sounds absurd. But the Bible describes Satan as a master deceiver, one who can "masquerade as an angel of light"

(2 Corinthians 11:14), someone who wants nothing more than to deceive people in the hope that they will *not* follow the one true God through Jesus. In this case Satan could be creating a vision of heaven to reassure the NDEr that, no matter what, they will eventually go there.

A Gift from God

The third possible way in which I believe people experience a heavenly NDE is that they are already believers in Jesus and have been promised heaven, so that's what they glimpse: heaven. That's direct and simple. No deception here.

Overall, however, as I've described, I do think there are two possible ways in which a person can have a heavenly NDE and be deceived spiritually—a gloomy and dismal prospect. One involves deception after the event, when the NDEr goes his merry way, unaware of the need for faith in Jesus. The other involves deception intrinsic to the event itself, a situation in which Satan disguises himself as a divinely beautiful and wise being and presents a false portrait of a heaven that is accessible to all.

It's my personal opinion that of all the heavenly NDEs, the majority are God giving people a chance to glimpse the after-life and receive his grace in hopes that they will establish a relationship with him, and that the remaining "heavenly" NDEs are second-rate, fraudulent "miracles" devised by Satan (Exodus 7: 10-13 and 20-24, Exodus 8: 5-7). I believe many Christians are falling for Satan's "trap" by throwing the proverbial "baby out with the bathwater" and deciding that all NDEs are deceptive instead of viewing them as amazingly powerful examples of God's grace.

Later in this book I will propose a post-NDE technique that could alter an eternally hellish afterlife for NDErs, should they choose to try it. This result could indeed be heavenly.

CHAPTER FIVE

THE DARK SIDE OF NEAR-DEATH EXPERIENCES

What makes an NDE distressing or hellish?

What does hell look like?

Can Christians experience hellish NDEs?

What do distressing NDEs teach us about God and the afterlife?

don't have anyone's personal story of a hellish near-death experience to share here. Disappointing, I know. I had a friend's NDE lined up for this chapter and he opted out, even with the use of a pseudonym and altered personal details. I'm not surprised. Reliving a distressing NDE isn't for the faint of heart. Even listening to my friend's experience the first time, years ago, I felt alarmed for him.

In the eight years I've been studying and researching NDEs I have personally heard only two hellish or distressing NDEs, along with perhaps three or four from speakers whose NDEs had been published. Each time I've heard one I've been amazed that the person was able to summon the courage to share it.

This brings us to a point worth mentioning. Hellish or distressing NDEs are highly underreported. Reliving such a terrifying experience takes a person's time, drains their emotional and mental energy, and tests their faith, if indeed they are believers. What if, at final death, they were to go to a hellish place again, even after adopting a loving lifestyle and redeeming spiritual beliefs? While I might casually ask the NDEr to explain what happened, I'm deeply aware that the experience was vivid and deeply troubling. I respect this. Going to hell in a near-death experience is a terror I've never known and have no wish to imagine.

I cannot even guess what the ratio would be of pleasurable NDEs to distressing ones. Published accounts of disturbing NDEs are far fewer than heavenly ones because people neither like to share them nor read them. But there are several relatively current, North American published accounts, including Howard Storm's experience recounted in his book *My Descent into Death*.

I read *My Descent into Death* years ago, and it has stayed with me. I called Howard so we could talk about his experience with a hellish NDE. He is friendly and serious about what happened to him. This is only a brief synopsis, and I encourage you to read the book for yourself.

A tenured professor and atheist, at thirty-eight Howard was awaiting emergency surgery when he experienced his NDE. Howard described floating above his body. Then, not knowing what else to do, he followed some beings who directed him to come and assured him they would take care of him. He followed them through a doorway into a dark, misty place. After a time he began to feel deceived and wanted to go back, but the beings turned on him, pulling him apart and eating him alive. They tore off pieces of his flesh and defiled and humiliated him in ways he stated he will not share with another soul.

While Howard was being tortured, an unrecognized voice within told him to pray to God—to the God he did not believe in. As he wrestled with this thought, the voice prompted him again. Howard began to pray to God to save him, along with repeating anything he had ever learned with God's name in it. The demonic creatures recoiled with each utterance. It was working. Eventually Howard saw a pinpoint of light coming closer and closer until it enveloped him.

What happened next is so beautifully moving and powerful that my words cannot do it justice.

Howard Storm met the person he didn't think existed. He goes on to describe how Jesus healed him, took him to heaven, shared Howard's life review with him, and answered his hard questions.

Many Christians have criticized Howard's book because they disagree with his theology. I can understand that. However, as I'll explain later, I believe it's important to listen to the experiences of people like Howard Storm, even if their theology may seem "off" to you. Discernment and distinguishing between spirits should happen within the body of Christ (see 1 Corinthians 12:10, 20, 27). In brief, God calls us to share each other's burdens and to be gentle with one another (Galatians 6:1–2), something especially important when dealing with someone who has had a hellish or distressing NDE.

Elements of a Distressing or Hellish NDE

What makes an NDE distressing or hellish? We know from research that there are several shared elements.

NDErs may find themselves in

- a dim or dark place
- a black hole, either physically in the ground or suspended in the universe
- a space of complete silence or nothingness, a void
- a burning, smoldering, fiery place
- a place of physical torture
- a place where they sense they will never again have meaningful contact with others
- a place inhabited by cruel, merciless, or deceptive beings
- a state of eternal confusion or deception

Finally, in a hellish NDE a person will often experience deep feelings of dread and hopelessness. They may believe that they have missed the chance for a different outcome, and they may mourn their previous way of life or their lack of faith.

What Hell Looks Like

Hell in NDEs is depicted in many ways, with the classic fire and brimstone actually the least reported. As I've already mentioned, however, distressing NDEs are the least reported overall, as they can be terrifying both to the NDEr and to those hearing the account. No one wants to experience hell, to hear about hell, or to believe in hell. Yet here hell is in front of us all, being shared by courageous people in our time, as well as warned about it in the Bible.

After much research I have come to the conclusion that all of these variations listed above can be biblical. The fiery pit described in Revelation 20:14 has also been described by NDErs. There have been accounts of people clinging to sides of a pit or hole; people finding themselves in a smoldering, sulfuric-smelling place; people feeling grabbed or clawed at by other people or beings; . . . and the list goes on—sounding terrifying with every variation. These NDErs often report that they knew this agony would be never-ending.

The more frequently described iteration of hell, of those who have reported, is an eternal and internal void. A place of nothingness. These destinations have been perceived as hellish, either instantly or gradually, as the person reaches out for knowledge, love, or contact but receives nothing but realizations of doom. One NDEr found himself suspended in a "black hole in the universe." Often the state of mind of the eternal nothing coincides with a physical experience the person remembers, like a pit or dark tunnel. This is not, however, necessarily the case, as it is often described as simply an awareness that nothing more will ever be possible.

So hell, as experienced in NDEs, doesn't have to be physical. The Bible describes this element of eternal separation in 2 Thessalonians 1:7–9:

> *This will happen when the Lord Jesus is revealed from heaven in blazing fire with his powerful angels. He will punish those who do not know God and do not obey the gospel of our Lord Jesus. They will be*

punished with everlasting destruction and
shut out from the presence of the Lord and
from the glory of his might.

Initially, the NDEr may not recognize that
the eternal separation is from God. Most do note,
however, knowledge of the everlasting absence of
all the great and wonderful qualities of life, such as
beauty and love. This loss is completely frightening
to people. If they do not have a previous
relationship to God, they might become aware
for the first time that such a personal connection
is possible, or realize that the God shared with
them while still in life was real and that they were
remiss in failing to find out who he was. If NDErs
have had previous faith but still find themselves
in a hellish NDE, they are often terrified that their
connection to God has been severed.

Deliverance from Hell

From what I have read about NDEs and heard
firsthand, someone who experiences a hellish
NDE never, thankfully, stays in hell; in fact,

God responds to pleas of mercy from believers and (erstwhile) nonbelievers alike. This seems to contradict what the Bible says about non-Christians who have not "chosen" to believe in God through Jesus before death. However, the fact that the NDEr didn't *actually* die reminds us that this wasn't final, physical death for them, though of course they didn't know that at the time. So, whether they escaped hell because Jesus appeared within the experience and lifted them out or they simply returned to their earthly physical state, they didn't stay in the hellish place.

I have a theory about this deliverance, but it isn't new and isn't mine. It's called God's grace. As I grow and learn about God, I realize how like him it is to extend his hand down into our messes and pull us out with the offer of a second chance. He has done that for me over and over again in my life. If an NDEr's prior worldly beliefs didn't include belief in God or Jesus and yet they were "saved" from doom, this suggests that God is granting another opportunity for them to enter a new relationship with him when they return to life on Earth.

Those people who have found themselves in horrible places and cried out to God to save them have had their pleas answered. In some of these NDEs awful creatures stopped torturing the NDErs after their repeated crying out to God. Speaking his name transported them to a safer, heavenly place, a place bathed in light. This next point is biblical and shouldn't be overlooked: calling on Jesus in any genuine, faithful way the person knows, or merely speaking his name, is complete power. In Howard's case, not having had a prior belief in God, calling out any name of God or Jesus, as he did in his NDE, and trusting God's sovereignty and power, worked. While this is deeply comforting, we have no way of knowing that everyone would choose to cry out to God in such a situation, or that the voice that prompted Howard (and others) to pray to God would also speak to them. There are too many unknowns for anyone to be comfortable or complacent in this situation.

Surprisingly, some Christians have experienced hellish or distressing NDEs. While a hellish NDE is understandably deeply troubling to believers, they may be able to come to an understanding of what they've experienced and even to share the reasons God allowed them to see and experience such a devastating place. Again, we must remember that NDEs aren't final, physical death, so a hellish NDE doesn't necessarily predict a hellish eternity. God can show a person anything he wants to. What the person decides to do with the experiences and information provided is up to them.

A Christian named Bob Taylor endured a distressing NDE but was able to process his experience and derive some important lessons from it—lessons that still reverberate in my heart today.

Bob Taylor's Story

Years ago my sister handed me some stapled papers given to her by a man, Bob Taylor, who frequently visited her office and knew about the research I was doing. "Look, it's his NDE." On the top was his name; the title; and a big, red, official-looking stamp that said "DRAFT." I have never forgotten his story. Over the years it has moved with us to different houses and acquired a coffee stain. I have read and reread it. As I worked on this book I tried to find Bob and discovered, to my surprise and delight, that he had submitted more than one NDE to a friend's web page that I could reference.[2] Contacting the friend, I was told that Bob had passed away; sadly, then, I was unable to interview him personally.

Bob's story and Howard's are similar in a few ways. After dying on a beach and then later at the hospital and having near-death experiences, Bob found himself walking, exhausted, down a dark corridor. A "soothing" voice beside him congratulated him for making it "through," and Bob listened to the voice because it "was

2   See http://www.wor.org/Books/w/A_Wake-up_Call_to_the_ Church.htm, "The Corridor."

everything you ever wanted to hear from someone."[3] The voice then shared that Bob would be disabled and blind if he chose to go back. But Bob explained to the voice that God wasn't finished with him yet. He referenced 1 Corinthians 9:23–27, about choosing to finish the race God had set before him. After a while he realized that the voice was actually his enemy. When Bob stated again that God wasn't finished with him, the voice and the corridor disappeared.

Both Howard and Bob realized that the beings and voices that were initially so helpful were actually deceitful and leading them toward destruction. From his experience with a hellish NDE, Bob concluded that spiritual battles for a person's soul may not be over after the person dies and that one must still be on guard to watch for deception and proclaim spiritual truth and belief in God when needed.

Bob made another astonishing point: "The enemy may know things that you are not yet

---

3   Ibid.

aware of."[4] Hemorrhaging would indeed appear later behind his right eye, endangering his sight. The voice had knowledge of Bob's current condition and of the condition to which he would return, and it lied in the hope that Bob would let his defenses down and resign his spiritual fate. In near-death, Bob had to choose to believe and profess that God had a plan for his life, even if he were to be disabled.

Conclusions

Where does all of this leave us? What I have come up with is this. Separation from God is hell, whatever that looks like. Although one can speculate all day about why a particular person may have experienced a hellish NDE, the NDEr gets to determine the reasons and the impact it will have on their lives. And from what I can tell, the God who rescued the people from the hell in their NDE is the same God who allowed them to

---

4   Ibid.

live and avoid experiencing physical, final death at that point. Knowing that, those readers who have endured a distressing or hellish NDE can still cry out to and count on that same God to reveal to them meaning, purpose, and hope in their lives.

In addition, distressing NDEs can remind us of the power of God's name. Having some additional or "inside" information about God, as in Howard's case, while physically on Earth is important, and having a relationship with him and knowing his plans for you, as in Bob's case, are even better. Howard was able to call upon Jesus to save him physically from a terrible place, and he ended up being "saved" spiritually for eternity. Meanwhile, Bob was able to recall his relationship with God, refuting the voice that was trying to deceive him into further darkness. Many verses in the Bible exhort us to call upon the Lord and be saved. Acts 2:21 declares that "everyone who calls on the name of the Lord will be saved." And Psalm 86:5 proclaims, "You, LORD, are forgiving and good, abounding in love to all who call to you."

No one should wait until death to call upon God. After all, no one is guaranteed an NDE or a space in between in which we'll be granted an opportunity to wait and see. Joshua 24:15 reminds us to "choose this day whom you will serve"— whether it's ourselves, prestige, wealth, power, comfort—or God.

I'll share one last story I found while studying what the Bible has to say about hell. It seems to me to fit NDEs as well, and it comes from Luke 16:27–31. In the story, a parable told by Jesus, a rich man ends up in hell because of the selfish life he has lived. There he converses with Abraham, whom he can see in heaven from across a deep chasm. He begs Abraham to send someone to warn his brothers, to go and tell them to change their lifestyles so they will not end up as he has. Abraham reminds the man that his brothers already have Moses and the prophets to teach them how to live a God-honoring lifestyle. The man pleads, "But if someone from the dead goes to them, they will repent," to which Abraham replies, "If they do not listen to Moses and the

Prophets, they will not be convinced, even if someone rises from the dead" (Luke 16:31).

Stories of hellish NDEs won't necessarily convince you of the existence of hell, heaven, or God himself. But through this story Jesus warns you and me to call upon the powerful name of God—while there is still time.

CHAPTER SIX

COMING BACK TO EARTH

What are the immediate aftereffects of NDEs?

Are NDErs completely changed?

Some of these aftereffects seem disturbing.

What does the Bible say?

Near-death experiences, whether heavenly or hellish, are fascinating to hear and read about. But possibly more important than the NDE itself is what happens to the person afterward. Sometimes the changes in the NDEr will be imperceptible to others, especially those who are not family members or close friends. But in other instances they will be dramatic.

Carol, whom we met in the first chapter, had her NDE while undergoing surgery. After her NDE she was denied extra time to heal and found that she could not return to her nursing anesthetist program, prompting a change in her life's direction. If you looked at beautiful Carol, you would never know that "something" had happened, physical or spiritual, unless she told you. Nonetheless, Carol changed dramatically as the result of her NDE.

Dennis, in chapter three, experienced his NDE after having a motorcycle accident in which his body sustained major physical damage, including the need for a tracheotomy. If you looked closely at my big biker friend Dennis, or heard his voice, you would be able to tell that something happened but not know what, unless he told you. Physically and spiritually changed, Dennis will never be the same.

What happens to someone after an NDE? According to *The Handbook of Near-Death Experiences*, many personal changes may follow an NDE, including:

- An altered perception of life, including new religious beliefs
- Changes in relationships, divorce
- Emotional changes, either positive or negative, such as decreased fear and anxiety or increased depression or fear
- Paranormal phenomena, including out-of-body experiences, seeing spirits, an ability to heal, precognition, telepathy, awareness of dreams, contact with spirits, and changed energy fields[5]

---

5 Janice Miner Holden, Bruce Greyson, and Debbie James, eds., *The Handbook of Near-Death Experiences: Thirty Years of Investigation* (Santa Barbara, Calif.: ABC-CLIO, 2009), 42–51.

This list is paraphrased and by no means exhaustive. Typically, the combined physical/physiological, emotional, psychological, and spiritual aftereffects completely change the NDEr, whether or not the change is noticeable to others.

As with any life-changing event, the NDEr's interpretation of what they have experienced often helps determine the impact of the aftereffects on their lives.

An Altered Perception of Life

Howard, in chapter five, experienced a complete life shift after his NDE, noticeable to any friends, family members, or colleagues. During his NDE he experienced remorse over the manner in which he had treated others, yet at the same time undeniable and intense love from God. God presented Howard with a new outlook on life, new views of himself as being loved and cherished and capable of showing grace to others. Howard received a new calling to go and share God. An outspoken atheist and professor before his NDE, afterward he became a Christian minister.

Like Howard, many NDErs come away with new attitudes toward life, not just a new perspective on death. NDErs report feeling more compassion, affecting how they treat the earth and animals; becoming more philanthropic; and becoming less critical of personal choices and the choices of others, chalking up mistakes to greater life lessons learned. A woman named Michaela said of her NDE: "It changed everything about my life, and that's not saying I was totally different after. I was still the same person, but it made me think about everything differently."[6]

Changes in Relationships

Carol's husband and Dennis's wife were both able to withstand the changes that occurred within their spouses and in their relationships.

---

6 Michaela's NDE can be found on YouTube at https://www.youtube.com/watch?v=jTcHWz6UMZ8 and https://www.youtube.com/watch?v=br9X7MYnqEs.

However, Howard's first marriage became a casualty of his post-NDE beliefs and choices, and he has since remarried. Relational estrangement after an NDE can be sad and difficult to work through. Unfortunately, this is not uncommon; both partners have a great deal to process, since the NDEr may have undergone profound changes that end up affecting the relationship as well.

A crucial time in the life of any NDEr is the moment they choose to become vulnerable and confide in someone else. How the listener reacts is critical. If the listener dismisses or minimizes the NDE, any future interactions may be strained, and the NDEr may shut down partially or completely about their experience.

Emotional Changes

NDErs commonly report decreased fear of the dying process, of leaving their loved ones behind, or of the afterlife. Most NDErs also report joy over the things they have seen and the promises unveiled to them, the fulfillment of which, once again, is still to come.

However, some NDErs may experience increasing panic, fear, and depression after what they've been through. These people tend to remain under the radar. They will not likely report this experience and may have a difficult time processing it themselves, much less sharing it with others. These negative emotional changes may be in response to having experienced a hellish place, a void, or even a "heavenly" place that just didn't feel genuine or "right" to them, as in Bob's case of the heavenly deceptive voices. These NDErs may return feeling doomed or lost, or feel as though they've been tricked out of the heavenly realm they had been anticipating. They may experience frightening dreams and may have a general feeling of unrest. The combinations of feelings and experiences are endless, because emotions, beliefs, and experiences are so unique to the individual. My heart breaks for those who are silently suffering in this way.

Again, most NDErs report positive NDEs with positive life changes. It's those voices we haven't heard, the voices of the people walking around feeling damned, silenced, or crazy that most touch my heart. To them I want to say, "Come out, tell me, we can sort out what's going on here, it's safe." I wish they would feel that same assurance from others, but as a movement sweeps through the church to discount NDEs and the people who have experienced them, I understand why they stay quiet. It's difficult to speak of things no one else wants to talk about, as we shall soon see . . .

Paranormal Phenomena

We've discussed how life can change for an NDEr and how many of them may react to an NDE in a very human way that most others can neither understand nor appreciate. But some aftereffects of NDEs are truly extraordinary, falling under the category of what we typically call "paranormal phenomena." Here's where the discussion gets even more interesting! Before you bail out, remember that reading about the paranormal isn't the same as practicing it or believing it to be true, and that by discussing the paranormal we hope to broaden our understanding and awareness of what has been documented to have happened to people. Normal people! Which makes what I'm about to discuss less "crazy" than you might think.

While researching NDEs over the past several years I realized that I have experienced some of these very things or even do some of these things in my life, although I don't call these experiences by their "New-Agey" sounding names. We need to be aware of what a phrase means to the person using it, and what the experience was like for them, because their experiences and definitions may be unique to them. I say this so that when you're discussing spiritual things with someone you've just met at church and they mention frequent "contact with spirits," or any number of other things related to the spiritual realm, you feel comfortable enough to dig in a little more and ask what that looks like to them. How much better this approach than immediately passing judgment that someone isn't a Christian, doesn't believe in God, or is practicing voodoo magic abracadabra! The person might just be unusually spiritually in tune! Examples, including personal ones to make my point, will follow.

Out-of-Body Experiences

More and more people are reporting OBEs these days, as social stigma might be lessened somewhat by the current wave of NDE reports being published. Knowing that our minds and bodies are foremost spiritual and not physical, it isn't such a leap to see how a mind/soul (not the physical brain) can leave a body. Many NDErs experience an OBE, or multiple OBEs, within moments of their accident, injury, or surgery. An extremely notable OBE/NDE combination, one of my personal favorites, was shared by Pam Reynolds, who was able to see her surgery from above her body during an operation called a "standstill." After having clicking devices inserted into her ears, the blood drained from her head, and her body temperature lowered to icy cold, she still accurately described a surgical instrument, as well as the conversation that took place among the surgical team while her heart was stopped and she was clinically dead.[7]

Michaela, mentioned earlier, experienced multiple OBEs during a coma following her accident. When the pain would become too great she would leave her body and go to different rooms of the hospital. OBEs can happen at the moment of the event but continue to happen afterward as well.

Seeing Spiritual Beings

Some NDErs report being able to see deceased people, spirits, or angels after returning to their new normal. The NDEr's terms might need to be clarified, as some angels look like physically

---

7   See https://www.youtube.com/watch?v=VUD6kfEcgLc.

normal people and not floating spirits. For example, Howard Storm continued to see angels for a while after his NDE. In a Christmas Eve email, he shared with me about the angels in response to my question about them:

> Merry Christmas, Tracy,
>
> The angels were beautiful, beautiful. Surrounded in brilliant white light that filled the room. They appeared to be all male but that is not certain. Radiant is the best description I can give. Yes, we talked a lot. They are very patient and kind. They encouraged me to have faith, hope, and love.
>
> Christ be with you,
>
> Howard

Personally, I would say that I, too, have seen a "being," what I will call an apparition. I was alone in our home while my husband was serving in Iraq and went to check on something in our guest bedroom. Immediately after turning the corner into our hallway, I was aware that I had just walked up to a whitish form of something either falling, floating, or suspended in the air in front of me, like shimmering particles that dissipated quickly as I walked through. It was visible enough for me to notice, think it strange, and then turn around to investigate whether particles of something were falling from the ceiling. I couldn't find a source for anything of that nature, nor did I find any particles on my shirt, or dust, or anything else that might have explained the sensation. The light coming in wasn't the afternoon sun that highlighted dust in the air, and the form was denser than that. This wasn't something I had sought out, but I did see it, and reporting it to you doesn't make me crazy.

Hebrews 13:2 declares that from time to time we might see angels or even "entertain them unaware." Although an apparition may be different from an angel, it is still part of a spiritual world to which we do not always have access but might bump up against occasionally.

But while we might encounter the spiritual world by accident, we are not to deliberately seek it out. Leviticus 19:31 cautions, "Do not turn to mediums or seek out spiritists, for you will be defiled by them. I am the LORD your God." The Bible says that we are not to engage in contacting spirits or the dead, probably because God wants us to consult him and trust him first and foremost with our futures. In fact, Saul was condemned when he called up the spirit of Samuel (1 Samuel 28). Yet the Bible speaks often of a spiritual world that is beyond our common ability to sense.

Some NDErs use spirit guides in their attempts to connect again with that spiritual realm that impacted them in such a meaningful way in their NDE. Some people even try to contact deceased friends or family members. I can see how such contact might be comforting or affirming, as well as exciting. However, God sternly prohibits these practices in Leviticus 20:6: "I will set my face against anyone who turns to mediums and spiritists to prostitute themselves by following them, and I will cut them off from their people." So I encourage NDErs to honor God's wisdom and instead seek direction, affirmation, peace, or protection through Jesus.

One final word about communication with spirits. It isn't wrong to have an angel or Christ-proclaiming "spirit being," for lack of a better term, contact you. If one has, and didn't seek it out (except possibly by crying out to God for intervention), this is biblically acceptable, if not completely amazing/terrifying/you fill-in-the-blank. God occasionally uses angels to communicate with his people and minister to them (see Genesis 16:7, Judges 6:22, and Acts 23:9). Even so, we must measure what this angel or being is sharing with us against Scripture and with trusted Christian friends. The apostle John cautions in 1 John 4:1: "Dear friends, do not believe every spirit, but test the spirits to see whether they are from God, because many false prophets have gone out into the world."

According to the Bible, angels have specific jobs with regard to us as humans, and they are fully aware of this Scripture command that we

not worship them or seek them out. If an angel
is being sought by conjuring, I would be highly
wary of the biblical nature of the interaction,
including what information is shared (see
Galatians 1:8). For while some angels serve God,
others are fallen and serve Satan (see Matthew
25:41; 2 Corinthians 11:14).

Ability to Heal

Another paranormal phenomenon that some
NDErs report is the ability to heal others.
After their NDE, many are overwhelmed with
compassion for others and by the sanctity of all life,
prompting their use of newly found gifts such as
healing. I've never met someone claiming to have
this gift, but it is reported by former gold-medalist
figure skater Adam Miller, who had an NDE in
1977 and has since devoted himself to healing
others.[8]

8　https://www.youtube.com/watch?v=YC33BRVu-v8 and https://
　www.youtube.com/watch?v=h2_EKtx6iE8 as well as https://www.
　adam-healer.com

Jesus is the first and best healer and redeemer, and the disciples who were close to him also demonstrated an ability to heal the sick (Matthew 10:1). Although it isn't so unusual to think that someone who has experienced an NDE, who was close to the presence of God, might for a time have the ability to heal, we need to remember that those early healers did all of it in Jesus' name and were quick to give him all the glory. And again, we need to remember to test any healer or prophet or teacher against the revealed Word of God. If we find that what they say or do contradicts the Bible, we should be wary of their teaching.

Precognition

Another paranormal phenomenon is that of precognition. NDErs may report an increased ability to sense that something is about to happen or may already have awareness of events to come that were revealed to them in their NDE. Many NDErs share that they were allowed a peek into the future to see events or people that will one day come into their lives. Often people remember these precognitions from their NDEs, but sometimes they don't recall them until they play out in real time. I still consider this precognition because they did know in advance, although they may have forgotten and been reminded of it.

At this point some might notice that the biblical concepts of prophecy and precognition seem closely related; they may even be different terms for the same phenomenon, identified variously by different groups. It's helpful to bear in mind here that prophets, those called to share future events or to speak God's truths, were given special instructions by God. The same could be said about NDErs sharing what was revealed to them in their NDEs. The line is very fine here with regard to wording, incorporating what the NDEr means and what the listener or reader perceives. To Christians, prophecy is biblically recognized as an accepted and God-inspired phenomenon, although some Christians don't believe in modern-day prophets or prophecies.

Other Christians do believe there to be modern-day prophets with words of wisdom from God to be shared with all. One thing is certain: prophets and prophecies must always be tested against the revealed Word of God, and the Bible often warns against false prophets (see Matthew 24:11, 23–24, 2 Peter 2:1, and 1 John 4:1–3).

Telepathy

Following their NDEs many people report the "purported transmission of information from one person to another *without using any of our known sensory channels* or physical interaction."[9] This is called telepathy. Those experiencing NDEs may be able to converse with light beings or angels without speaking and are often surprised at their continued post-NDE ability to read minds.

Absent of "help" from spiritual realms I'm unsure of truly telepathic exchanges between humans, because in human form the slightest of

---

9   http://en.wikipedia.org/wiki/Telepathy, emphasis mine.

bodily cues can be sensed even subconsciously in a nonverbal exchange. If you think about it, many people have what might be called telepathic exchanges every day, though they wouldn't necessarily call them that. Most often these can happen between people who know each other very well, like spouses and siblings. For example, my husband and I can open the refrigerator, each of us thinking about what we might want for dinner. He can pick something up and look at me, and I can look back at him back with virtually no expression to indicate that we might be communicating. Yet we are, and he might put it back because I "said" no and then reach for something else. Within seconds the alternate selection might be agreed upon, though without verbal or any other overt communication.

I say that to remind us to ask what *telepathic* might mean to someone else and what telepathic communication looks like to them as they experience it, Many, if not most, of us can communicate in a way some might deem to be telepathic.

Do I believe that true telepathy (communication without using any known sensory channels) can happen between human and human? Maybe. But, if so, the communication would definitely fall within the category of paranormal.

On a somewhat related note, I believe that I have *truly* telepathic exchanges every single day, multiple times a day, between myself and the Holy Spirit. This is not in human-to-human form but is instead human-to-spirit, and such dialogue is perfectly normal and indeed encouraged by Scripture. According to the Bible, the Holy Spirit is the third member of the Trinity and the part of God who indwells a person's soul from the moment they've expressed their faith in Jesus (see 2 Corinthians 1:22) and become a Christian (see Galatians 4:4–6).

The Spirit leads a Christian in a very real way, often communicating through their thoughts. He is what people mean when they refer to "Jesus in my heart" and affirm this as "a real relationship." For me, this telepathy looks like a continuous commentary that often defines or even defies what I'm thinking or what I desire in my heart to do or say! Sometimes I "hear" instructions or the words of a Bible verse. Sometimes I sense a nudge to go and share something with someone words I've been told by the Holy Spirit to say— words that leave the person flabbergasted because they thought no one "knew" their circumstances. Christians all over the world can attest to this form of soul-speak. It is biblically promised to all who are believers in Jesus Christ, and the relationship is amazing. It grows just as person-to-person relationships do, only it's person-to-Holy Spirit—and vice versa!

Dreams

Many NDErs share that they have an increased awareness of dreams and that the information gleaned from them affects their post-NDE lives. Dr. Mary Neal, in her book *To Heaven and Back*, wrote of a post-NDE dream in which a young boy came to her and told her that he had "traded

places" with her son in death. Years earlier, when
her son was very young, he had told her he would
never reach 18 years of age because that had
never been the plan. This shocked her. Years later,
during her NDE, an angel spent most of the time
preparing her for her son's future death and for her
ongoing role in supporting her family. Sometime
after her NDE, and during a post-NDE dream,
Mary listened as an unknown boy inform her that
he had taken her son's place; she felt somewhat
relieved by what she construed as the prospect
that her son might be spared after all. The next day
she learned that a local boy had been killed in a
wreck and, sometime later, that her son had also
been killed in a devastating accident. God may
have been using the timely words from her son, the
NDE, and the post-NDE dream to prepare Mary's
heart for this tragedy. Mary undoubtedly was more
acutely aware of her post-NDE dreams and the
insight they might hold, demonstrated by the fact
that she was alert and waiting.

Not all post-NDE dreams corroborate the
spiritual understanding or themes within the

initial NDE. Carol, the OR Nurse in chapter one, shared with me that she had experienced many "disturbing dreams that came to pass" before her NDE, so she was not a stranger to listening to her dreams. Nevertheless, she went on to state that her awareness of dreams and the meanings or messages within them did increase after the NDE. At sixteen she had been warned that she or her sister would die in a car accident. Her sister did indeed pass away years later at thirty-five from a car accident. Although it wasn't through a dream, God spoke to Carol saying, "I love her unto me." The phrase puzzled her until she learned the terrible news of her sister's death and realized that God had been assuring Carol that her sister was safe with him. Carol was prepared in another dream for her unborn son's cleft lip, which came to pass as well. Carol has learned to listen and pray about the meanings and outcomes of such dreams. Despite tragic news that might have elicited anxiety, both Mary and Carol have shared the Bible's good news that we do not have to be anxious about or afraid of what is to come,

and that when we seek him the Lord will give
us strength in the hard times (see Psalm 23 and
Philippians 4:6).

Although some of the following points about
dreams are not in conjunction with NDEs, we
can see that dreams are often a unique spiritual
pathway for all of us. Many times in the Bible God
has given people visions or messages through
their dreams (see Pharaoh's in Genesis 41:8,
Nebuchadnezzar's in Daniel 2:1–11, and Joseph's
in Matthew 2:13). Although not all dreams are
filled with special instructions to be interpreted
or messages to be shared, this is a repeated form
of spiritual connection in the Bible that, in my
opinion, can be very valid, while unique for each
person.

Sometimes deceased people "visit" others in
dreams. Close friends, people I know and trust,
have confided in hushed tones that loved ones
have visited them in dreams after their passing
away, either with special messages of love and
comfort or in the form of bursts of love-filled
light. I know that this must be happening to many,

many more people than those who have shared with me personally and in privacy. This is amazing and exciting to me. We shouldn't demand special dreams or use spiritists to provoke them, but I believe that we can take comfort from them when they do happen. I even at times humbly pray that God will give me a comforting dream, especially when I'm feeling sad or missing someone. I suspect that, more often than not, we don't receive things from God simply because we don't ask. When, from time to time, he does grant my expressed request, I am amazed at how he did it and can't wait to share the experience with others.

One of our family friends had a dream about her mother that helped her in a unique way. Her mother, who had passed away years before, came to her in a dream and taught her the secret family gumbo recipe her daughter had never had the chance to learn before her mom's passing. My friend awoke, was able to replicate the recipe, and was inspired and thankful for the "visit" from her mom.

Changed Energy Fields

Some NDErs report that something physical must have changed within them; they've noticed it when they couldn't wear a watch or work with electronics such as a computer, because it kept breaking down. Are you ready for my amazing explanation about why this happens . . . ? Sadly, I don't have one. In my research I have reached out to some very smart people in an array of applicable fields . . . and found none who could speak to this. I didn't have to look hard online, however, to find that this is a reported phenomenon for some people who have had an NDE.

So what do we do with that? Here's my opinion. Just because I can't explain something doesn't mean it isn't happening or that it isn't impacting the person in real ways as they move on to live their lives. If someone can't seem to keep a functioning watch, experiences consistent breakdowns with electronics, and identifies this "dysfunction" as being followed by a spiritual experience, I can only imagine that scenario to be extremely frustrating and highly complex to work through. It might even cost them their jobs or relationships as they try to explain it to others, and they may feel jinxed or doomed. How would anyone explain all of this and try to overcome it, or at least work with it? I have to ask myself how I would behave toward or support the friend, family member, or coworker who confided in me about this. I think this is the more productive question here.

Visions

Visions are certainly unique and spiritual and beyond us, "transpersonal," as some might call them, because they are by definition beyond the person. But biblically they are a valid and documented experience, separate from dreams (see the book of Revelation). Sometimes a person will have a vision during, or only during, the NDE; in other cases these visions first occur or continue to happen to the person post-NDE—

which is our focus in this chapter.

Bob, the NDEr who "died" on the beach and then again at the hospital, had a vision during his NDE and again while recovering.[10] During his NDE he felt as though he had been "caught up" into heaven like the apostle Paul in 2 Corinthians 12:2. Then, during his recovery in the hospital, he was awakened and shown the words of Psalm 23 written on a ticker tape that scrolled past him at varying speeds. He was able to focus on certain parts of the verse and to interact with a voice that encouraged him to seek a deeper understanding of the meaning of the psalm. As Bob demonstrates, the NDE can happen as a vision, or one can experience visions after the NDE.

Compassion and Wisdom Required!

Again, the reason I spent time examining paranormal phenomena is that these things do

---

10 http://www.wor.org/Books/w/A_Wake-up_Call_to_the_Church.htm

happen, and they do affect people's lives. Because
we are called to love one another and be in
relationships with other people, we need to be
able to discuss all spiritual matters, not just the
ones that seem comfortable, "normal," or socially
acceptable. People shouldn't be shamed into
silence about having had an NDE or an OBE or a
vision or supernatural visit. We need to exercise
compassion and wisdom in order to respond
appropriately to others and not to shut them
down.

However, I want to encourage each of us to
examine paranormal experiences through the
lens of the Bible, because the Bible itself addresses
these spiritual and supernatural events. There are
some downright strange experiences recounted
in the Bible, as there are some downright
strange experiences I have shared in this book. If
paranormal phenomena happened in the Bible,
they can—and I believe do—happen now. But just
because such a thing can and does happen doesn't
mean we should deliberately seek out paranormal
experiences. God himself has already shown us a

better way to experience the spiritual world.

One final story should make my point. I once
attended a conference on death and spirituality
that offered a breakaway session about learning
to use a scrying mirror to contact the spirits of
loved ones. I was intrigued enough to quickly
look online to find out what this was all about.
I learned that scrying was an ancient practice of
looking into a reflective object, such as a crystal
ball or mirror, for the purpose of seeing a spiritual
vision or hidden message.

Here's the deal. I believe that scrying likely
works. I would have loved to have been a fly on
the wall to see what happened in that conference
room! What spirits did people see? What did
those spirits say? How did this impact the person
scrying? I say "would have loved," because I didn't
go. As I pointed out earlier on in this chapter,
God has drawn a line against practices like
scrying. If we love and honor God, it's best not to
have anything to do with acquiring information
through improper channels.

But God's rule against consulting spirits isn't

the only reason I didn't attend—nor was it the more compelling reason! The biggest reason I didn't go is that the knowledge and wisdom I receive from the Holy Spirit every day *far exceeds* anything I could ever receive from a scrying mirror. I can ask for comfort, wisdom, and even direct insight from God and have every confidence that the insights will be granted to me in a more powerful and personally meaningful way than by any other means I could employ.

And here's the best part: whatever answer I receive or whatever I learn won't just be good for me personally but will enrich the lives of everyone who gets to hear it. Nothing—this insight included—will return to God void; its meaning will bless and be blessed, and all because I simply asked. In the words of Proverbs 3:5–6, "Trust in the LORD with all your heart and lean not on your own understanding; in all your ways acknowledge him, and he will make your paths straight."

People shouldn't be shamed for experiencing paranormal phenomena, any more than they should be shamed for seeking out comfort through activities like scrying. Who wouldn't want to see or hear their loved ones again? But people need to be informed that their paranormal experiences demonstrate the existence of a spiritual world, including a God who has something to say about how best to interact with that world. In fact, God sent his Son, Jesus, just so that we could connect with him. Through the Holy Spirit we have an awesome spiritual connection with a God who can literally make anything happen.

So if you or someone you know is spiritually searching after an NDE, I would advise you to steer away from scrying and reliance on mediums and spirit guides. Instead, seek out what is undeniably spiritually healthy: an authentic relationship with Jesus.

CHAPTER SEVEN

RESPONDING TO NEAR-DEATH EXPERIENCES

Why we love to hear about heaven

Why many criticize near-death accounts

How we get to respond

love to stand in line. I know. Totally weird. The longer the line, the better. Christmas at the mall? Fantastic! I love watching people. What they do, or don't do. How they choose to present themselves. As a group therapy specialist with an undergraduate degree in sociology, I'm fascinated by people's reactions, their subtle body language, their choices on how and when to share who they are and what they think, and what others do with that information in return.

When I tell people I research near-death experiences, I don't miss their reactions, and, as you might expect they are varied. I see the people who nod and give a polite excuse to leave the room and the conversation. I see those who for a fleeting moment wish to engage and hear more but think better of their gut reaction and self-monitor, remaining polite and quiet. Then there are those who find it impossible or inappropriate to hide their scorn, for whatever reasons; such individuals may loudly share a verse, such as 1 Corinthians 2:9, implying that we can't possibly know or imagine what God has in store for all of

us, and with a tense laugh effectively shut down
the conversation. (Interestingly, they almost never
share the verse immediately following that one,
1 Corinthians 2:10, which states that God reveals
such things by his Spirit.)

And then there are those remaining few people.

I see them give me a quick glance, right in
my eyes, searching for trust. The gaze is fleeting,
and later on they hunt me down and schedule
a time to share their experiences. I'm invariably
amazed at their bravery. If such encounters sound
dramatic, like clandestine meetings, it's because
they are. Up to that point the person may never
have mentioned their NDE to another soul, for
fear of harming their reputation or of others
questioning their sanity. Or, worse, they may
have opened up about it to friends they trusted
and been shut down or shamed. Worse still is
that person walking around feeling damned, or
trying to reconcile their experience with their
spirituality, or utterly confused, trying desperately
to make sense of something they've seen.

How I Respond

"I know you're going to think this is crazy," or "I know you're not going to believe this," or "I've never told anyone this" is most often the beginning. I can assure you that these people are most often high-functioning, down-to-earth individuals. People at your church or grocery store. People like you. People you may know.

My reaction is encouraging and open. I listen and affirm. I don't have to agree or disagree with the theology I'm hearing because that isn't my aim. My aim at that moment is to be with them, to understand what the NDE meant and still means to them. I'm in awe when they are. Scared when they are, as they retell their stories. I watch their breathing and their excitement to see how extraordinary the experience was for them, how foreign it still seems to them, or how shocked they still sound when they express their wonder at why this has happened to them, "of all people."

And the experiences are incredible. My aim is for each person to keep relating their experience until they think they've covered it all. This may take a few hours or even days! I've discovered that once a person has established trust with me, and following their initial recounting of the experience, I might continue to get phone calls or texts at all hours as they discover what something might mean or what plans God may have for their lives. I encourage this. I listen to them telling me how amazing and freeing it is to be heard, to get it out into the open, to be affirmed so they can use their unconventional spiritual experiences to move forward. I'm even more encouraged and excited when they share that they aren't ashamed or afraid anymore, that they might even want to share their story with a group or write their own book. This is a victory.

I also feel the tension when someone who has had a hellish experience describes how they lived their lives before the NDE and what there was within the NDE that helped them see what they could do better. These are heart-stopping, life-changing events. And I wait at the end, hoping they will share having found a way to make sense of it all. At times I gently ask this question, and sometimes the answer is no. They may say that they have, but sometimes their actions and words suggest that they have not. This is troubling. And let's not forget that NDEs often accompany a traumatic event, such as a car accident or a near-drowning. These people have lived to tell about it, but going back to talk about the experience isn't always easy. They have struggled and anguished and grieved lost loved ones, former lives they knew, ongoing lives they'll never know, or limbs they've lost. These individuals are precious lives, souls who are still here with us. Sorting through an NDE and its effects is often an overwhelming process, both for the teller and for the listener.

Why We Love Stories about Heaven

We love stories about heaven. Just look at the bestseller list of the last few years. *Proof of Heaven* by Dr. Eben Alexander sold nearly one million copies in 2013 alone. *Heaven Is for Real* by Todd Burpo and Lynn Vincent has sold more than a million ebooks and more than 10 million hard copies since 2010, and *90 Minutes in Heaven* by Don Piper and Cecil Murphey has sold more than six million copies since 2009. That's millions of people buying and reading accounts of heaven. Many curious individuals simply want to see what the hype is about, but others love the topic and can't seem to get enough of it.

I think that people love the topic of heaven because it represents, on a basic level, hope for a different realm, for something more, for some amazing destination where wonderful things await us. Heaven represents for most love and peace, and for many the place where we'll meet God, . . . and who isn't interested in that? Meeting an all-knowing and loving Creator? Yes, let's experience that. People are curious.

Why We Criticize Near-Death Accounts

People usually have one of two reactions to hearing about an NDE. Either they are amazed, inspired, and awed by the account or they are fearful and critical, worried that the details of the NDE are not in line with their beliefs about the afterlife. It's easy to criticize experiences we don't understand and people we've never met. In fact, I think the pendulum has recently turned from readers reading and loving stories of heaven to their viciously attacking the authenticity of the experiences, as well as of the people claiming to have had them. I understand the questioning. Critical thinkers, discerning people want to understand why NDEs don't always make sense, why many seem fantastical or why only certain people claim to have had them. They wonder why these accounts don't corroborate with Scripture in a literal way. I don't know these answers. But I can appreciate the drive to know. It's good to think critically. But just because something doesn't make sense to us doesn't mean it isn't real or hasn't really happened. Mind-blowing occurencess, indescribable, can't-believe-this-is-what's-in-store events are after all God's forte. This is night-before-Christmas exciting to me. What isn't exciting to me, and what I feel needs to be addressed as our society currently struggles with the whole concept of NDEs and spiritual experiences, is this . . .

How Then Do We Respond?
A Call for Compassion

In 2010 Kevin Malarkey and his son Alex coauthored a book detailing Alex's car accident and his ensuing near-death experience. Titled *The Boy Who Came Back from Heaven*, the book became an immediate bestseller. Sales continued to climb until January 14, 2015, when Alex issued a public statement confessing that his story wasn't true. In response, Tyndale House Publishers stopped printing copies and Lifeway Christian Stores pulled the books from their shelves.

I'm shocked, saddened, and even angered by the ordeal surrounding *The Boy Who Came Back from Heaven*. But not shocked, saddened, and angry for any of the reasons you might expect. It isn't that the NDE might have been fabricated and ultimately needed to be retracted. I'm shocked, sad, and even angry at the way "Christians" responded to the account over and over again, before and after the fabrication came to light, on comment threads and posts all over the Internet, TV, and in conversations. From verbally trashing this child's purported experience to trashing him *as a person* to making fun of his name—all of these insensitve reactions floored me. Whole churches laughing, even mocking.

> Sit for a moment.
> Just take a moment.
> Picture it.
> Feel the gravity of this.

If I were an NDEr, desperately seeking an unknown but newly-revealed-to-me God, I might think that *surely* this spiritual event falls under "church" (because that's where God is . . . right? And those Christians are loving like the Bible always says . . . right?). I might seek out my local congregation (any denomination or Christian group will do because that isn't my concern, after all. I've lived through a humbling and life-changing experience, and this God spared me and left me with a hunger to know him, so I go and find a church).

I might slip into the pew feeling unsure and strange to begin with with new people. And then I hear it: that no one "should" believe any strange spiritual experiences. Ever. "They aren't in the Bible. They aren't from God." "Those people who believe them are destined for hell for sharing such unbiblical, heretical stories and leading people away from God." I might not be able to leave fast enough. I most certainly wouldn't want to talk to any of the church members about the way to know God more, as they laugh and agree with the fact that it's all "malarkey." I might even feel stunned, knowing that God had spoken to me and that he had worked miracles in my life and given me the chance to live again for him, but at the same time I'd feel utterly devastated and confused at the open shunning from my "brothers and sisters in Christ." I might not pick up on the shaming and silencing tactics, but I would certainly feel them. And I might feel lost all over again. Dreadfully lost. I might leave that church, the place where Christians are called to worship, and seek out a different way to God. It certainly isn't going to be through Christ, if that's how Christians act.

If that isn't sadness inducing I don't know what is. Yet I suspect that this is happening all the time. Far more often than we are aware. Yet what can we do? I would respond that we "should" do the things on the list below, but counselors cringe at the "should" word, and for good reason. I like the verb phrase "get to" better. I think it fits. If we get to be here on the Earth for even one more day, if we get to encounter other precious souls who are seeking God and long to know him, if we get to choose to hear their stories because they're important, then when we as Christians hear accounts of NDEs we can follow these steps:

1. A Christian *gets to* listen.
2. A Christian *gets to* be open to learn.
3. A Christian *gets to* search the Scriptures.

4. A Christian *gets to* affirm the person for bravely sharing the NDE.

5. A Christian *gets to* share the path to God through Jesus. A Christian *gets to* share that receiving Christ is a free gift that no one has to—or indeed can—earn or be good enough for. A Christian *gets to* join in glorifying Jesus together with the NDEr, or just walk beside them in friendship as they continue to try to figure it all out. We *get to*. It's a privilege.

6. A Christian *gets to* stand back and be amazed at all of God's work, all of his children, all of our experiences, knowing that there is so much more than we have ever imagined waiting for those who believe in him.

Conclusion

In a previous chapter I mentioned my intention to share a foolproof way for NDErs and others listening to them them to bypass the uncertainty of not knowing whether their experience was or was not "from God." I mentioned that I would share how someone could be *sure* that whatever happened in their NDE wasn't given to deceive them and lead them down a path to destruction. It's simple: commit the whole experience to God. Thank him for whatever it was that happened, even if God wasn't the author of it. Whether the experience was completely heavenly, heavenly though parts of it felt a little deceptive, or completely hellish, we might not know what to do with it.

That's okay. It's okay not to know. But if God allowed you to experience it, try to learn from it. Give God the credit for being the Creator of all things and for loving you enough to show you a powerful glimpse of who he is. Pray, asking him to show you what you need to know, based on the experience, and how you're supposed to move forward from this day on. Praise him and thank him for another chance at living. Thank him for Jesus, who promises life in heaven to those who believe, and humbly request the loving guidance of his Holy Spirit. He will lead you to where you need to go for more insight and further growth (perhaps he has even led you to this book!).

Still not convinced that God is involved in NDEs, or that belief in Jesus is crucial to experiencing a heavenly afterlife? That's okay too. We can still be friends! Although I must say that crazy things that we can't explain happen every day. Near-death experiences and other spiritual events reveal to us a world we can't grasp rationally or scientifically, but a world that is nonetheless revealed and explained to us in the Bible. In fact, there is a passage in the Bible that seems to describe near-death experiences—and how God uses them. You'll find it in Job 33, which I include here as my epilogue—without comment or commentary because I want you to experience the incredible power of God's Word on its own merit, and how God might speak to us at the times when we're most vulnerable—when we're asleep, injured, sick, or even dying.

I think that God has been showering the Western world with these extraordinary NDEs

for reasons bigger than you or I can understand.
He has once again been using dreams, visions,
and near-death experiences to enable us to see
him. He has made these NDEs unforgettable,
with amazing scenery, the revelation of incredible
insights, and beautiful portrayals of his love. He is
bringing people to himself and prodding millions
to start talking about the afterlife through heart-
to-heart conversations over coffee, at bedside
visits with dying loved ones, and via internet blog
post comments. When we respond to NDEs,
will we see the bigger picture? The seeking and
the finding? Will Christians stand in the way of
God's reaching out to the people he loves, the very
people he came to save? I hope not. I pray not.

AN INVITATION TO THE LIGHT OF LIFE

Job 33:12–30

"God is greater than any mortal.
Why do you complain to him
that he responds to no one's words?
For God does speak—now one way, now another—
though no one perceives it.
In a dream, in a vision of the night,
  when deep sleep falls on people
  as they slumber in their beds,
he may speak in their ears
and terrify them with warnings,
to turn them from wrongdoing
  and keep them from pride,
to preserve them from the pit,
their lives from perishing by the sword.
"Or someone may be chastened on a bed of pain
with constant distress in their bones,
so that their body finds food repulsive
and their soul loathes the choicest meal.
Their flesh wastes away to nothing,
and their bones, once hidden, now stick out.
They draw near to the pit,
and their life to the messengers of death.

Yet if there is an angel at their side,

a messenger, one out of a thousand,

sent to tell them how to be upright,

and he is gracious to that person and says to God,

'Spare them from going down to the pit;

I have found a ransom for them—

let their flesh be renewed like a child's;

let them be restored as in the days of their youth'—

then that person can pray to God

    and find favor with him,

they will see God's face and shout for joy;

he will restore them to full well-being.

And they will go to others and say,

'I have sinned, I have perverted what is right,

but I did not get what I deserved.

God has delivered me from going down to the pit,

and I shall live to enjoy the light of life.'

"God does all these things to a person—

twice, even three times—

to turn them back from the pit,

that the light of life may shine on them."

ACKNOWLEDGMENTS

I am so very grateful to the following people for their belief in this project and for the efforts they took to help it succeed. To my husband, **Jonathan**, thank you for being so inspiring and creating calm in the chaos of our lives so I could write. You're nothing short of amazing. To my precious daughters, remember our secret. To the NDErs who shared their stories with me, you are so brave to share, and I'm so proud of and thankful for you. God bless you. To my parents, **Bob** and **Sharon Holcomb**, and my sisters **Elizabeth O'Neal** and **Beth Bridges**, please know that your insight and attentiveness were crucial. I can't say thank you enough. To my fellow NDE enthusiast and cousin **Paul Marshall**; you are so loved. To my mother-in-law, **Shirley Goza**, and my brothers and sisters-in-law, **Jeremy** and **Staci**

Goza and **Joel** and **Sarah Goza**, as well as to my church family at Houston Northwest, thank you for cheering me on and for being kind enough to listen and give feedback.

To **Dr. John Townsend** and **Sandra Vander Zicht** for referring such an amazing writing coach, editor, and friend in **Lori Walburg VandenBosch**. Lori, my process with you was exceptional, and I have grown immensely from your instruction. Thank you! Thank you also to **Howard Storm** for sharing your story with me over the phone, and especially for your servant's heart. Thank you to **Bob Goff** for living *Love Does* and for being available for ten inspiring minutes on the phone, and to **Kent Marshall** and **Justin Ray** for taking time and trying to explain scientific concepts I still don't completely understand. You're geniuses!

Thank you to each friend who took the time to proofread the manuscript and provide feedback: to **Mark** and **Mary Morris**, **Michelle Bennett**, **Dr. Steve Bezner**, **Kelly Maier**, **Dennis Shea**, **Carol Garrett**, and others. To **Katie Rogers**, thank you for listening to me dreaming aloud and for helping in such a hands-on manner to make so much of my dream come to fruition. You are truly "Katie the Great!" A huge thank you **Tim Beals** and his amazing team at Credo House Publishers. This book became a reality only because of your hard work.

And finally, a thank you to treasured loved ones who have left us in death but remain alive in Christ:

My grandparents:
Mildred (1996) and **Ernest Marshall** (2005)
Thank you for barefooted days and for letting me ride around on the lawn mower. Thank you for teaching me about Jesus and showing me what it looks like to serve others. I miss everything about you: your voices, your hands, your smiles and laughs, your stories, your charm together as a couple, and your cozy cedar house. Sometimes I feel you near or smell your perfume or pipe. I miss our being together.

My Grandmother

Eppie Holcomb (1998)

Thank you for living with us and for teaching me what it looks like to honor parents and grandparents, even in sickness and death. Thank you for showing me your brave spirit while fighting Alzheimer's and for trying to make our home pretty by putting in a surprise rose garden so you could see something calming and beautiful during your hazy and confusing days. Thank you for letting me be with you in your hospital room at the end and for allowing me to experience, as a young person, the absolutely holy feeling of death. I felt your spirit leave. I want to know you so much better when I join you. I love you.

My Aunt

Warrene Marshall (2008)

Thank you for loving me in your gentle way and for sharing time with me right there at the end. I wholeheartedly believe you saw that rabbit creature that no one else could see. Those present saw the look on your face and sensed the peace in your soul while you watched it. I miss you and can't wait to know you adult to adult. I love you.

My Father-in-Law
Roger R. Goza (2014)

I'm so glad your granddaughter saw you in her bedroom after you had passed away at the hospital. Her insistence that she saw you as you are now— "running, laughing, and joking"—when she was too young to know to say that, comforted us and still gives us hope. We love and miss you. Thank you for mustering up the energy to talk business with me that night when every word was hard to speak, and for such encouragement. Thank you most of all for your hope and faith in Christ and for passing these qualities along to your son. I miss the sparkle in your eyes.

My precious nieces
Junia Hope Goza (2014) and **Phoebe Grace Goza** (2014)

I didn't get to hold you or kiss you when you were delivered, but I promise to do that when we officially meet for the first time. Aunt Tracy loves you.

Peter-the-Pug (2011)

I had no idea that a little soul could claim so much of my heart. You were a delight for ten years, seeing me through Jonathan's deployment to Iraq and through all of my morning sickness. You were so brave while battling cancer. I miss your velvet ears, searching eyes, and long tongue every day. You taught me about patience, faithfulness, and unconditional love. When I get to heaven, I want to see you first.

Each of you showed me what it means to live and die honorably, love unconditionally, and seek God's face. You strengthened my relationship with Christ and left in your absence an ache for an eternity more of your spirits.

I love you all and *can't wait* to see you again.